Berries in Abandoned Lots

A Poetry Collage

Edie Eubanks-Fields

First Edition, First Printing

Printed in the United States of America
Edie Eubanks-Fields, Des Moines, IA

ISBN-13:978-0615596785
ISBN-10:0615596789

Library of Congress Control Number
2012902138

To You

For Joyce and Tony

We are repository for the other. Cherish our collective self.

Love to Tony and Crystal

Of all your alliances and imaginary friends, you're my favorite.

Gratitude to Diane Foster, whose words, "*Sure* you're a writer," spliced new thought, and took me in a direction outside of writing within my own privacy. I remember you.

Contents

Part 1 - Synapse

Contents

Part 1 - Synapse (continued)

Contents

Part 2 - Dusty Album On the Back Shelf

Contents

Part 2 - Dusty Album On the Back Shelf (continued)

෨൬

1

෨൬

Synapse

Numb

Followed old-wives' advice...
        ...way beyond the bride-price...
...Fold away sacrifice--
        it will keep on ice.

ഓൽ

Post Graduate Degree of the Valedictorian

I'm in the bush-league,
an underachiever breed,
desiring neither gain nor lead,
having neither goal nor greed,
earning all the gruel-fatigue...
conferred when you don't succeed.

ഓൽ

Dazed

Butterflies flittering, gyring
        among the lofts...
Wasps summering, hiving
        in attic posts...
Bees bustling, vibing
        in rafter joists...
Fireflies flickering, jiving
        inside my gourd...
All blinking, choiring--
Va-cancy--Va-cancy--Va-cancy

Signs of Life

I suppose I could have stayed that way
and gone on and expired,
which is where I was headed,
that being the fate of middle-agers,
that, or going wild.

Being too conservative, too straitlaced,
and too anal retentive,
which has always been my downfall,
going wild was out of the question--
and so, began an overhaul.

Going wild *would* have been yes-yes! fun,
but scan'lous and unchurch-like,
and of course unmother-like,
(but certainly wife-like),
but...sigh, I'm unlike that.

So Real Life just took a hold of me,
jerked me around,
kicked the juice out of me,
whipped my behind, and threw me in bed writhing,
where I signed and shook,
and curled up sucking my thumb with my eyes closed,
and lulled off into a Long Sleep,
never combing my hair, and getting rounder 'n rounder.
And dreamed, till I heard the alarm sounder:
awaken from your darkened cave,
you've had too many years of hibernation,
too many years of frustration, too many years of time-wastin'.

I suppose I could have remained like that
and gone on and expired,
which was easier--
that being my fate,
that, or going haywire.
But, I dragged myself to the cave's mouth,
and decided I *wouldn't* go on and expire,

--expiring being the choice of anyone with common
    sense--
but instead, I'd stop stagnating,
and procrastinating, and vegetating.

Being sourceless, and jobless, and clueless,
having buried myself in this little town,
which was my main pitfall,
what to do not to expire was the big question--
that, and nothing more at all.

I knew I'd have to go further than the cave's mouth,
so I decided I had to step out into the sun,
the sun being where I needed to go,
in order to feel any new sensation,
to effect actualization, to begin re-creation.

Going wild *would* have been wu-hoo! fun
but scan'lous and unforgivable,
and of course, unlivable,
but definitely agreeable,
so I went wild,
and started writing.

So Real Life took a hold of me.

ଔଓଷ

Seen Hanging in the Dream Gallery

Traipsing lightly through a field of Queen Anne's lace
    in billowing chantilly
and ruffled chiffon parasol,
near a fence where fairy wash sunned,
        and paper-winged lepidoptera lit;

meeting another,
    in airy, cream camise and milk seersucker and panama,
    extending a babies'-breath bouquet.

Bluegrassland

Amid eagle-flown, cedar-grown pleasure,
spanned over three nature-textured miles,
we fingered sensory-tingled treasure
along gritty, dirt-wilderness aisle;
wow!-green and tree house-seemed
within clustered, heavy-leaved boughs,
folding us in from verdant rich sides,
beneath pea-spinach, tea-sheen clouds;
concealing deep in fern-tinged fable,
tale-lost children, ooglin', bug-eyed,
beneath an ivy-fringed table.

     In tinied distance, tan path converged;
branches showed through tree'd verdure,
and overhead green merged
like a trellis, wreathed of glee'd-allure,
conjuring a tom thumb wedding procession,
with gold-burn sun, and scorched milk sky
surging blink-twinks in latticed succession.

Hidden birds trilled high, flutey, piccoloey songs;
a long one whistling sterling melodious tones.
Len mimicked silvery notes.
All birdsing hushed.
Crystal, fluidly-lilt throat
subtled a sly touch.
Len echoed the weald-hid flute.
And then *we* shushed.
Melodic jousting ensued--
     we, tingling, tittering,
     with each ascents' twittering.
Piercing song climbed
in crowning resonant key.
Len couldn't stretch-rhyme...
Birdland breath-held quietly...
then Len re-tried--
phrasing new-pitch do-re-me;
     the scale master snubbed him in silence--
     air quiet-hung, in bird-league compliance.

Bursting into mass laughter,
and loud voice-melee,
we jabbered in noisy, awed chatter,
and continued on sunny-shade way.
Leftward, mazed, lush underbrush
vine meshed and jungle dropped
a wild-thrust, entangled bluff,
landing bare and belly-flopped
along shore-washed, sandy mush--
      tree-fallen, fallen-leaved,
      rock-cluttered, broken-debrised.
Muddy river, in silent flow below,
was seen only when woodsy leafage thinned;
when honeysuckle and briers bowed low;
then whispered--only as we paused again,
      listening for quiet lapping and swishing,
      while hordes-inspected by in-the-mouth kissing
of unnamable, gnat-fragile, flying thing-gies,
and tiny dwarf, greeny-milk moths
with delicate, flickering, little wing-gies.

Plush, dextral-thicket gave reign
to sparse, shade-roofed woods
enthroned in dark, moundy terrain;
its shadow-forest, beech-maple-stood,
among floor-grown roots and purslane.
Sun-danced canopy of lolling breeze
gold-squinted above pebbly ranged trail;
over rough campyness of crashed trees,
while beer cans, butts, broken bottles yelled,
      screaming amidst rich, pure untameness,
      spoiling and soiling beauty, claimless.
Cross pass--a treacherously-worn strip--
dived left, and pitched us headlong,
as we stumbled, slid, flailed, and slipped
down to slush-muddy shored-home
      of snake-squattered, doodoo-green water--
      then clawed back up; not fools, or martyrs.

Thickets eased, while trail right-squeezed
a sweep of slate rock-face and fallen shards,

stretching forward dark as seas;
climbing craggy, airy yards,
        clenching fingerly overhangs,
        root-surviving on cliff-hooked fangs.
Scrunched vein-like and feral beneath,
meager, grassed pass single-filed;
broken slate lay jaggedly-teethed,
huddled crushed in slidden piles,
        hosting marching, stomping feet
        while thousands-crunching underneath.
The towering, scowling wall--
jots of scrubbage wracked with wind
jutting from its cleft-rut sprawl--
hemmed ribbony path tightly in,
        torturously, tapering trekkers left,
        wild-becoming, with each step-slide step,
indistinguishable, trailless, impassable ground,
as we inch-crept, heel and toe,
atop movable, smunchable, platy mounds,
and eyed the rock-toothed drop below.

ৡৈৈৣ

Kingdoms

I touch the tunes of Spoke-flung things,
from awesome halls of blues and greens;
I kiss the hues, and tongue the smells,
of earth-tinged brown and air lapels.

From crystal spurs in dark-hued sky,
to rock-notched floor where gemmed beds lie,
to sedge-flesh stems on stream-damp shore,
on these sight-fruits I gorge, and more.

With still-stopped rays of sun-gilt slants,
which stream through trees on work-bogged ants,
and glass-bead drops on rain-glist' leaves,
I wipe my mouth on earth's green sleeves.

The grace-dressed leap of white tail stag,
through fern and grass of glade and quag,
and soft rain-veils which bathe hushed-elms,
are jeweled earls in nature-realms.

Rich kingdoms mix their own sweet juice,
and finger-paint the plush blue spruce,
or daub the soothe of crickets' songs,
or splat that loud cicada-throng's,

Or splash blood-smocks of hollyhocks,
near quaker-ladies' blue-tone frocks,
and brush gold manes of dandy lions,
'neath green, bowed heads of willows cryin'.

I drink it all, this flush highball,
then romp beneath its alcohol.
I whippoorwill in eve's cool light,
and yell my name with kook bobwhite.

I race through briers with cottontails,
hopscotch sparrows on woodland trails,
crawl through tunneled, gnawed-out mazes,
sculpt by feeding-white-ants' crazes.

I'll strum thriving echo-niches,
wear ballooning Dutchman's breeches,
waltz the washing, ocean wave-dance,
sip magnolia's dizzy fragrance,

Sing the marsh-spring watercresses,
wake up nodding ladies' tresses,
chomp the famous, fabled moon rocks,
grope the tangled, brambled boondocks,

Ear-sniff wiggly, woolly squirmers,
scare the whispered, rustled murmurs,
cool the tranced moths at their singeing,
when I'm stuffed tight--I'll stop bingeing.

In dew night-quiet, I'll belch out loud,
then fall asleep in moon's white shroud.
At dawning's yawn, I'll gulp my fill,
of morning glories' twining frill.

Hidden Intricacies

She thinks he's into her...
She's just an unasked extension of his tower room,
like a black-basked tomb,
a shatterproof space to enter...
with guaranteed protection,
a soundproof place to lie down--
Lying, with no detection,
a foolproof base to remain...
forever, a disconnection.

ဆာၢ

Love-Ache Song

Love song of the thorn-barb thistles,
Love song of the burr-sting spurs,
Quilled with all your piercing missiles,
Rhymed with all your bristled slurs;

Trill of how you cut to marrow,
String of how you steel your dart,
Music how you pang your arrow,
Straight into love's bull's-eye heart.

Strum your stab-and-slash tale of me,
While you sharp your pare-blade knife,
Peeling slowly as you love me,
Tonguing as you raze my life.

Whet-kiss gently as you spear me,
Chord the thrust of your next strike,
Edge the lance as you death-shear me,
Hoist my head upon your spike.

Tears

Laughter's tears--
  damp and wiped

Joy's--
  spontaneous and light

Emotional's--
  embarrassing and unfeigned

Sadness'--
  snot-run and unwaned

Pain's--
  few and restrained

Heart's--
  uncontrollable and inconsolable

Beytrayal's--
  hot

బుు

Renewal

Stripping off the capes of dreamers,
Ripping off the cloaks of schemers,
Snipping cowls of low-esteemers,
Youthed, she made a choice.

To the well of her emotions,
Like the swell of gentle oceans,
As a spell of calming potions,
Soothed his tender voice.

Late

I was blind-driving
her outmoded, road-glut tank
because she
was too Seagrams-drunk. She was too
out of it
to tell me
how to get Jennine from work.

I drove down wrong-said
roads, down wrong-pointed
dead-end, to woods-lined, dark
road-wind that led up a mountain
climb, then we turned back again.

She wasn't too boozed
to hate-spew that her father
had abused and blood-beaten
her will-bruised mother,
over long
hell-dwelt-years;
how she hated him, how she
man-fought him whenever
he misused
her scare-ruled mother.

Between cruel episodes
of her bent, bastard father,
she'd liquor-rage yell from
back of the narc-car,
as though *my* wires were crossed;
as though we were mired and lost
because *I* was rot-gut sauced.

As I Braille-guess drove,
she slid-scoot-rolled
across the backseat,
reliving from hell's hole
--soaring high--

slurring out hate-him
tales, slapping the back
of my seat, raising the peak of
my-annoyed, fearing Jennine'd
be ranting-schizoid
because she was so repeat-late.

And then, from some space
somewhere, for some reason
in the air,
it came, from inebriate safe place within,
"Eade, I'm a lesbian."
...*as though I didn't know;*
If she'd been *half*-sober,
we could've close-dialogued,
but, she wasn't,
she was stone-grogged, and I
stole baby-sit-glances
through rear mirror, while I tried
thinking clearer, about
our muddled circumstances.

"Did you hear me?!" punched
her gin-voice, "I said--
I'm a lesbian!..."
She needed me to *say* something,
leaving no bigotry unvoiced.

"That's okay," was space-
said. I couldn't share-talk
the back of my head, not knowing
which way to turn-keep
the wheel; megaphoning loudly
through her binged buzz cloud,
to her fogged brain-veil.

"You don't care?" she voice-
strained, "you don't care
that I'm a lesbian?!"
I found her in rear view mirror
again,

where she also found her
way...our spirits sliding nearer...
"it's all right, Payton...it's *okay*."

I wasn't yea-yeaing
her life-style,
I was yea-saying her worthwhile;
saying I already knew,
knowing--I still cared. She
was my near-neighbor, she
was post-tall, she
was man-dressed, she
was boot-camp crewed.

I enjoyed her company—
having gone fool-down, fool-road
a couple of huh?-times before
on some wild-goose, sucker-chase
romp, but she hadn't been down and
dumps-drunk, and I hadn't been
bumbling blindfold
down fool-never-drove roads...

...I wait-stood
behind Payton, at walled pay
phone, three years flown-
gone, not knowing it was her.
Finishing...she hung up,
stumbling to motor-clipping
cab, as some-familiar
quiet-whispered, "there..."
I turned,
cruising the glassed eyes...and
was shock-fried.

She'd Been Washed Away...
care-shrunken in height
as well, faded to model-small,
and rinse-spun
on hell.
She didn't know me in her

haze, or even know I was there,
she was so drinkdrug-dazed.
I hadn't seen her forever.
I knew Jennine had left her.
I knew she'd lost her job...
and the house.
She was too transformed for
any aloof to stay calm, and
hurt, still-stopped tears
gathered and sad-laid, and
throat-heaviness
you can't swallow, came and stayed.

The dust-cab pulled off.
Legs unmoving ran after it,
Mouth unspeaking shouted, "wait"!
Heart aching
wondered where it was taking her.
Eyes brimming,
noiselessly cried her hurt.
Mind telepathing, mustered to
thought-tap that she wasn't alone, that
there was someone--a friend--with
whom she could grieve and moan.

...I condemned myself,
why couldn't I
have told her all along?...
when I heard her
all the while,
say-weeping Jennine's impending-gone,
telling of a coming crashing,
warning of now/child pains gnashing,
letting her inadequacies
leak, letting her mask melt,
letting her guard slip, letting
her life-bred loneness seep?

Why was I
neither available nor accessible?...
...because...

of just-to-here walls...
because...it was *their* business...
because... I stood on the shore,
watching her gasp-splash, watching
her gurgling without sound, seeing
her SOS thrash, but witnessed her
death agony...
only after she'd drowned.

৪০০৪

Not Always Wholehearted

The bighearted aren't always
    the goodhearted
        or the kindhearted
            or the warmhearted

The heavyhearted aren't always
    the stonehearted
        or the iron hearted
            or the strong hearted

The weak hearted aren't always
    the chickenhearted
        or the softhearted
            or the tenderhearted

The brave hearted aren't always
    the stouthearted
        or the proud hearted
            or the truehearted

Of Months We Can Count on Fingers

Place bayonet guilt and dagger pain,
carousel sorrow and woodshed shame
(of these cry-months we can count on fingers
with *if-only* taste which weeps and mingles),
in a quiet steel box with a loose-fit lock;
and we can wound back, and we can stop
to long-gaze it later, or, whenever,
so we'll be able to say we never
pushed it pin-quietly under a rug,
then glibly denied it, like a secret-use drug,

but now, we have to move on,
or we will bleed here forever.

∞○∞

Wishes and Cream

Wishes...and the demise of need and expectation--
No, the *killing* of need, the pounding of it into quiet...
The corpse of dreams lowered into cried out desires;
The loneliest of burials, feeding on worms, to eat away want;
...Finally, resurrection--not anew--just final,
...devoid of life...undeclared dead...

        I envisioned flowery flowers,
        and sunshiny sun.
        I conjured cream and clouds,
        and sugary rum.

        I spun candlelight beaus,
        and magic moon dust,
        I sought rings, and roses,
        and all that stuff,

        And all I found was us.

tapestry

damask   cashmere   flannel

silk   wool

tweed   angora   muslin

velour   percale   velvet

serge   kente

suede   denim   linen

jersey   mohair

mackinaw   chambray   herringbone

you   do   them

all   a   favor

Programmable Robotic Chant

We live in a synthetic world
        inhabited by synthetic people

We glide down our synthetic courses
        and turn in our synthetic abodes

We contact our synthetic systems
        and review our synthetic events

We consume our synthetic nutrition
        and imbibe our sensorial libation

We approach our symbiotic mates
        and perform our synthetic syngamy

We produce our synthetic micros
        and discard our synthetic defectives

We obsess on synthetic substances
        to alter our synthetic states

We're absorbed in our synthetic operations
        which feed our synthetic existence

We oblate to our lords of syndication
        which rule our synthetic world

Sticks 'N Stones

"I hear you're aberrant."

           "Heard you're a sycophant."

"I hear you're really sick."

           "And you're a lunatic."

"You plastered maniac..."

           "...You sanctimonious hack..."

"I hear you like perversion."

           "I hear you lack conversion."

"You never pull the shade."

           "You hide beneath charade."

"You spill ev'ry what n' why."

           "I hear you're bred to lie."

"Ignorant..."

           "Arrogant..."

"I hear you're a FREAK."

           "But you'd rather SNEAK."

"I hear you're friggin' weird..."

           "I hear your mind is seared..."

" ... "

           " ..."

Dey Cole

Dey real cool. Dey
    lef school. Dey

deal dope. Dey
    chill hope. Dey

get rich. Dey
    dig ditch. Dey

roll strapped. Dey
    get capped. Dey

sell def. Dey
    kill sef.

ᾴᾷ

Courage Under Fire

"I be tryin'da figga out things all the time,
prob'bly nobody's as wo' out as I'm.

"She be growing up so fas,
and the food an' stuff never las.

"I need somebody to help when I hafta be gone,
cause I don' wanna leave her here alone.

"Wish I could find a wayda make money an' stuff...
when you ain' got nobody, it be rough...

"...Maybe somebody got some cash I could borra,
'specially wit' this one on the way.
...I be fifteen t'morra...
but--I be okay."

Will It Die by a Stake through the Heart or a Silver Bullet

Hopin' in the sixties we would have gotten over it,
but now is here, and it's Alive and breedin'.

Responding to its presence like those who read Braille,
but it's there before us like a bong bong bell.

Still callin' straight hair, *good hair*,
as though woolly hair's no good.

Sayin' "he's black as tar, *but he's still cute*,"
as though looking good *and* being black-black
is a thought that has to be forced to mind,
and when it is, it's only as a second thought.

Thinkin' light eyes or green eyes are cuter than dark eyes,
and throwin' him to the curb cause he's too blue-blackafied.

Bustin' your buns to get pregnant by the right Mr. Right,
so your baby--"will come out light."

Brothas talkin' bad about sistas, cause of how sistas act,
when sistas act like they act, cause of how brothas act;
And brothas runnin', cause they can't stand,
the hellified creations of their own hands.

Thinkin' soft white silken is more pleasin'
than soft black coarser, cause you can't stand
what's in the mirror, and in the bed when you turn over.

Lettin' our children on playgrounds and at the table,
repeat in voices of the past (and yours they heard yesterday):
"you thick-lipped nigga," "you wide-nose sucka," "you ugly black
thang."

Listenin' to our own comedians make jokes that murder black-
esteem,
relegating *dark* blackness to a state lower then *being* black

("...wit cho' black Miles Davis self..." "...wit cho' black Hostess Ding Dong self..."), haha and we laugh.

Hatin' the white man, with oh-so-fractured psyches,
for hatin' our blackness,
when we are hatin' it so ding dong well ourselves.

ംൽ൩

Keepers

Substance free, and free of feenin';
clean-pee-clean sobriety, setting you free of the reins...
　　　　　　　　　　　　　　　　...except your keepers'...

Cowled and powerful-
psychological testosterone, keeping your balls in a vise

Armed to the hilt with chains-
sexual opium, addicting to perversities

Unrelenting and merciless-
eating slaloms, burying at every turn

Growing and possessive-
greed bacterium, spreading fingers around your throat

Pinioning, and blowing smoke up your nose-
delusional delirium, asphyxiating in egomania

Calling all the shots-
tyrannical tantrums, trapping in maniacal vendettas

O,

that men could newly from our Oldland come,
with hope-eyes from wise-men sessions in thatch-roof hut,
untransformed
to street corner gather-loiterings with glass in brown sack,
with dried leaves in clear bag,
with crystal-powder from watched-labs;

would come with hunt-spear for boar-food and eland,
unmetamorphosed
into gray, steel-gleamed gun of black and yella, tan and brown-held
hands,
that stalk black and yella, tan and brown other men;

would move beyond the old tribal wars
that white and pale men smugly say is our heritage
of raged bloody in-battles of lines and turf,
who forget the clannish wars fought in cold misty lands,
and the ones fought here in street with tommy gun
in blood-run bistro,
which mowed down other white and pale men, whose grandsons
now wear wall street robes and carry *Fortune 500* bibles,
who have not wisdom to remember
they fought like Crips and Bloods, gangs and tribes,
for bootleg, snatch, and numbers.

O, that berry-skinned men would newly from kraals
and compounds of fathers-land come,
and move beyond
the beaten psyches, culls of the bottom and shantytown and ghetto
that milk-skinned men ride past,
and wag and disdain and deride berry-skinned men for
--for *living* in their incarceration--
and do not wish to remember that their milk-skinned fathers
marked the train-track lines of bottom-shanty town,
and drew grid-line of project-ghetto penitentiaries,
daring them with scare of law, of gun, of torch, and lynch, to inch
beyond,
until their spirit-roots connected with the separated ground...and
mutated.

O, that soul-torn men of weary, collective pain
would love their women,
would forgive their women
of too much will, of too much lip, of too much fight,
of too many dreams,
and remember their brute-soiled women birthed and toiled,
nurtured and reared berry-skinned babies
when red-stain, milk-skinned system prevented *them*;
would gather their children to them, and hold their women tight.

O, that royal sons' sons, and warrior-hunter sons of sons
would turn their guns into pen, and scalpel, gavel and wisdom
of dark-men-run universities of life-learning, power and earning--
or, would just *learn*...

O, that dark-skinned men and men-youth
would esteem life-richness
of black-skin kin
above blood-green lucre
of street corner drive-through bisness,
of school yard treats--or trick,
of where-is-my-money-bitch
Slavery:
would fulcrum powerful-talented-gifted
into no brother murder-harm,

would funnel rage into *Over*, ghosted-gone,
would up-lead brown ones now down-dragged,
and would have memory to recall
the past *communal* uplifting of dark-skinned kindred by other dark-
skinned kindred;

would lead themselves out of black-on-black darkness into light,
alongside wisdomed, dark-skinned torch keepers,
--would become mentor-keepers of torches--
like perpetual million-man marchers,
gathering in wise-men hut-sessions in mason-block centers,
in brick leader-leagues, dispensing council-wise lead
for whole village-good, of black-berried women and children,
and of other dark-skinned royaled men and men-youth--
transformed--
and from our old land newly come.

Down the Aisle

"Dearly beloved, we are assembled here..."
Smiling, teary-eyed pastels,
rainbow-sherbet birds, nodding in rows,
glad celebrants more of Weddings than of Marriages.

"...a most solemn, sacred and serious union..."
Arrayed backs carrying dead carcasses;
soon to make one another do penance
for untried crimes of others.

"...not knowing what is before you..."
Hearts cracked and insulated,
trying to join pastly-slashed veins;
a trail of bleeding already at the altar.

"...henceforth you will belong to each other..."
Money-Chase Mistress, Rainbow-Chase Dreamboat,
necessary lovers and time-occupying diversions--
tranquilizers against familiar pain--and each other.

"...one in mind, in heart and affection..."
Hide-and-seek hearts on watch-and-keep-score patrol,
to protect and serve self,
cruising on *destroy*-next-villain alert.

"...do promise and covenant..."
Shallow-breathed, limited guarantee vows,
clutching built-in disclaimer clause,
not mouthing standard open return policy.

"...to have thee, to hold thee..."
Embraced bodies, pleasure-satiated;
emotions, unhugged and starved,
while silently, hungrily pleading.

"...in prosperity and in adversity..."
Minds at ease and content in fatness,
not geared to endure leanness and threatenings,
ruminate that excess fat can be easily trimmed away.

"...to keep myself unto thee and unto thee only.."
If-you-work-out-if-you-don't-hurt-me-scar-me-cross-me-
if-you-prove-acceptable-satisfactory-suitable Trust,
Secretly reserving if-I-don't-lose-interest-or-find-someone-
else-like-they-did-me Options.

"...forasmuch then as you have consented together..."
Divergent self-preservationists with separate agendas,
craving love, not wanting to love,
needing to validate self, and to show *them*.

"...I do pronounce you husband and wife..."
...Gladly doing penance for all their sins,
taking you, your crap, your kittens,
and all your other kin.

ೞೞ

Sensate Melody

If you were touch,
     you'd be black velour
       draped kissingly against my skin.

If you were taste,
     you'd be the dark juice
     of tangiest fruit.

If you were scent
     you'd be the sunrise walk
     in swarthy damp woods.

If you were color
     you'd be hues of warm brown,
     and shades of cool, misty blue.

If you were music
     you'd be sweet-sad music,
     softly played.

Remember Crying to *Her* in the Night?

Paint rank, pissy stench,
gag-filth,
sepsis,
fecal crap--
in wastebaskets
on toilet seats...
under her nails;

dab brown crud around her mouth;
dip the brush in spittle,
and dribble down her chin;

pencil hair sprouting on her face,
thinning on her head;

fill-in "toothless"...
crepe paper wrinkles...
saggy skin;
sketch baggy arms...
hanging breasts...
swaggy butt, dish-rag flappy;

add no color or shape
to the drabwater dress,
spindly legs and body;

chalk
stooped,
hunched,
ugly;

blend in
ugly surroundings,
ugly care,
uncaring;

finish with
unloved,

lonely,
miserable,
abandoned,
distressed,
grieving,
inward weeping;

then hang it, where no one wants to hear.

ಐസಿಐ

Night Boy

He belongs among the plush covers galore,
the thrown, clean clothes on the floor,
the amp-funked guitar,
the rendered posters decor,
Rubik's, his poems in the drawer,
his Barnes and Noble hoard,
the on-line pretender-friends rapport,
the skeleton--which hangs near the globe,
that he can't go back to anymore...

He lives with the claws, the paws,
the mouths, fatigue-jaw,
the kneel-floors of rolling cars,
the dirty paper, flagged over glass ajar,
the steel grips, the rammed rods,
the ice cold walls, the protest scars,
the evenings, the alley czars;
the thin jacket, the one pair jeans.
And when he finally lies down,
he doesn't dream.

Upper White Blues

I'm a dazzling flare,
filtering through brightest light,
streaming over glass and lives--
a sparkler of blinding brilliance.

I have the mint,
for the schools,
for the couch,
for the cultural endowments,
for the high tech toys,
for the Swiss secret,
for the Columbian monkey,
for the Caribbean incognito,
for the Mediterranean hideaway.

I'm a backer,
an inside tracker,
wading in intrigue
and manure
in knee-deep boots.
I feel the squeeze,
I stretch the truth,
I milk the lies,
I snatch the rug,
I pull the plug,
I squeeze the triggers.

I fear the crash,
I fear the crowding,
I fear the browning--
the judgment--
them.

My father was my abuser,
way into the night,
my mother was my user,
sucking away my life.

My mate is screwed;
my life is a complicated hell.
My children are twisted,
but we hide it well.

I know it all,
except the answers.
I have it all,
except the peace.
I control it all,
except my life.

I want it to be differently
than what it is.
But God that I don't revere,
I don't want to be like them--

them--those--
shadows crawling down blackened alleys against the wall,
sloshing through the puddles,
lusting for the trash,
scroungey cats running through the dark, grappling, while
they try covering themselves with the night.

Walking the Floor

He was up again at 2:00 a.m.
dragging his chains
through the house.

He went to the frigidaire
to scope it out,
then to the couch
to channel surf in the dark.

He mindscaped once more
through the snow jobs,
around prefab dialogue,
and past stone dead replies,
through eyes that swam in suspended mist.

In agony he returned to the bedroom,
pushed open the great iron door,
and stood strobing inside the room,
flickering on the gentle breathing of tin charade.

He turned and closed the door softly,
and heard the heavy clanging
of metal behind him.

Caveat Emptor

Some of the smiles come plastic wrapped,
and some of the goodness is spritzed;
all veracity isn't vacuumed sealed,
and, packaged with peel back faces fastened with Velcro,
is meant to deceive and dissemble in every way.

₧₨

Where??

...at the end of the gun you've placed
in your mouth...
with his finger on the muzzle,
begging you not to squeeze,
telling you that he is;

at the bottom of the glass,
whispering that he can;

in the dive where you trick,
holding your inner child;

in the coven where you witch,
gathering you in his arms;

in the dump where you hit,
wrapping himself tightly around you;

on the bench that you've staked,
sliding close to you;

at the end of your rope,
giving you his hand.

Third Tangent

He's the odd man out,

not caring for women.

...or men,
not like that...
but he craves their company,
he needs to feel their presence,
he needs to be warmed by them, to be held by them,
he needs them to tell him it's okay.
But it's never happened that way...
...He doesn't really try to get close anymore.
The going price is high.

There is no place for him.
He doesn't belong anywhere.
There is no third option,
no brotherhood of odd men out,
nowhere he can go to be held.
A woman can't help him,
a woman didn't damage him, didn't brutalize him,
and a woman can't heal him.
He can't even love her,
until somebody loves him back from the damned.

From the depth of his scarring,
should have evolved a horrible Thing.
He has raged, he has wrestled, he has hidden.
What he has become, he feels, is...a non-thing,
wrapped tightly so that he won't feel,
while they all think he's a zombie;
or in private, becoming wildly unraveled,
and screaming like a banshee,
because he *needs* to feel.

He's not welcome in the real world,
he can't place the ad he's desperate to place:
"Straight man seeking straight man,

for intimate, non-sexual relationship."
Responses would come, he knows,
from those real-man types,
who feel obligated to call him pussy;
and from those who are looking for something
other than what he's said
...who don't believe he means what he says.

He lives on the edge of desperation.
He doesn't believe it will happen,
but he watches everyday,
for some friend who will hold him for free.

ಬಂದ

Post-Graduate Offer

The money's sweet...
...heavy, bad-boy secrets to keep...

        ...may need to marry your priest...

Can get...reasonably good sleep,
...with blood pooling beneath your feet.

Out of the Dust

When the house fell on me,
I was young, bright-eyed,
trusting...and lame.
When it pinned me under its heavy lumber,
I thought I'd never feel again.

Forever I pushed those beams away,
and planks that buried my head.
The pain was immense, raw and intense--
and after a while, it went dead.

When I healed, I'd toughened.
Nothing would wound me like that again.
...And the next time the house fell, like a bombshell,
I didn't feel the cave-in,

is what I should be able to say,
but that is a monstrous lie.
I bled more, worse than before,
contending with more than a black eye.

I struggled amid the rubble,
pushing away beams more heavy and mean,
mending more crooked and hollow, having more to swallow--
a house is a heavy thing.

The next time the house falls,
wet will cover my body,
my pulse will run wild and extreme.
I'll try to look bland, dusting my hands.
A house is a heavy thing.

Feeding Time

You...
without a thought--
think mine.

You...
without a mind,
I have a piece for you--
eat up.

You with no guts--
follow my droppings.

You...
with your head on backwards,
--over here--
my flank...lick.

You who like others
to nuzzle you from behind,
hold still--
let me piss-spray you with my scent.

You without the use
of your soul,
with your conscience
at you back,
and your brain in a bowl--
here...fetch.

You...
with your say
tucked between your legs,
who let dominance
rule you,
your meal is ready--
come eat it from my mouth.

Try

You're not going *anywhere.*
I've already scratched
your skin, and released my toxin
        beneath the welt.

        The nail you stepped on--was me.
and before you hope,
  there is no anti-ism.

        You were bitten
by my jagged-edge bite moons ago,
and malaise continues to spread,
        even now.

        ...The nausea you feel...
botulism I've fed you
        from my own hand.

        You might as well be still
and lie the way I want you.
        You can groan and twist,
You can retch and heave,
        I've already laid my eggs in your body.
...and you're not going *anywhere.*

Flicking the Switch

The moral glitch,
occurring in Christian moralist---

Minimizing a small "fraudian" slip,
        permitting an immoral hiccup,
            disguising corrupt eccentricities,
    normalizing spiritual idiosyncrasies,
        accepting sequined debris,
        covering hi-rank chicanery,
                spinning prevaricated labyrinths,
        spreading "gospel" verbal viruses,
            living as morally eclectic,
    in regard to "thus saith," anorectic,
        forgiving and forgetting verbatim,
committing adulterous mayhem...

Ahhh...the moral glitch,
available, at the flick of a switch---

୫୦୯ଓ

In Lamb's Clothes

                        Hateful
the hatchings beneath French-net brim.
                        Jaundiced
the rove behind expertly applied shadow.
                        Cannibalistic
the falsity between refined red lips.
                        Treacherous
the web in fashionable milk organdie.
                        Jugular
the deed in elegant sheer gloves.
                        Vicious
the errand of designer nylons and stylish pumps.

Sharp
the smooth blade knife--the Elder's wife.

Game Over

I've just ricocheted
behind the barricade
at the town arcade.

At Lee's Esplanade
is where I fell, touchéd,
by the game I've played.

It was I who preyed,
began this strange crusade
that the rules forbade.

Now I'm dossiered,
studied and cross-filleted
by the scoop parade.

Inside's all frappéd;
my bowels are loose- puréed,
and my brain's flambéd.

Life's not ready-made,
not for the renegade,
with Ruger and blade.

There goes tape-blockade,
'cause they are run-afraid
of the mess I've made.

Tales will be crocheted,
and I will be portrayed
as the priest who strayed.

There's no accolade,
nor even serenade
due this escapade.

Curtains custom-made
for death to intergrade,
will at noon cascade.

Shame I'll go in suede,
in smelly blue pomade,
and a monked-up braid.

No more masquerade,
or life in deep charade
since my mores swayed.

Plans won't be delayed;
at twelve the forms invade
past the palisade.

I can hide in shade,
and trounce the motorcade,
as they escalade.

When it's all been weighed;
when all muck wags have brayed,
then they'll post my grade.

It will be conveyed
my mind had long been frayed,
and my creed mislaid.

I've breached hell unbade;
I'm falling un-maydayed
into fires mine-lade.

This is over-played;
how 'bout a standoff trade...
for my launch-grenade?

Felonious

Adroit at jimmying emotions,
through lyrical duplicity
and rhythmical complicity;
seducing, confusing...
the master gimme gimme.

Adept at feeding needing,
with bogus, quasi-real,
serving empty liar's meals;
bruising, abusing...
the gyp gimme gimme.

Skilled in camouflaging scars---
quintessential chameleon,
loosing a sensual hellion;
rusing, excusing...
the angry gimme gimme.

Amateur in *shallow* caring,
not even becoming flesh to tom--
Does your nose grow with your phallus
as you penetrate so callous?
using, refusing...
the lifer gimme gimme.

Road Test

She soared,
test-driving her power,
each time becoming more reckless,
pushing every button on the loaded dash,
foolishly flipping every
glittering boomerang.

Her parents,
orged in a fugue state,
were ruling in sleep mode
...with spineless tough-love...
on such low dosage, she considered
it biodegradable.
They didn't have a waking clue,
they were just trying to slow drag
without standing up close.

This, and the fact
that she could smell herself,
cranked her into mouth overdrive
quite often of late, way past
any implied airbag protection
she might've had in the past.

But she had a gun-it-to-the-extreme
infatuation for anything,
and constantly served revved wolf-cookies
--which they swallowed--

and learned to shift into psych-
a-trol, and run them over
again and again with their own
guilt spasms, until she had flattened
them into tolerance-submission,

snoozing them on cruise control
    when they'd try to regain equilibrium,
then double-orge them into
pentothal-compliance.
--so it appeared---

She loved those power tunings
on the road. She giggled inside
and thought she was hauling gas
in the fast lane, not sensing, as she
floored, that she was idling on crash.

⊗⊙⊗

Mood Essence

It hovers
over asleep cities where ships blow in harbor,
where the Ripper and Hyde snatch the victim and ladies scream,
and Holmes chases to the wharf's water.

Around steeples it wraps, and flattens, and backstrokes,
and kisses panes cool wet,
dropping sheer veils over blinking lights;
transforming towns into late-intimate.

It drifts, and fades, and enshrouds, and conjures;
it breathes romantic, mysterious fantasy,
until I swerve blindly 'round that curve
and almost French that tree.

A'blowin'

the wind on the rise
on move through the skies
was a'howlin' an' a'hoohin'

an' the clouds on the move
at speed to a groove
was a'fleein' an' a'scootin'

an' the lines on the pole
with ripples on a roll
was a'movin' an' a'groovin'

an' the bird on the post
with still like a ghost
was a'quiv'rin' an' a'shriv'rin'

an' the roof on the shed
on hang by a thread
was a'rumplin' an' a'bumpin'

an' the gate on the hinge
with bangs on a binge
was a'flappin' an' a'whackin'

an' the grass on the ground
with lack of a sound
was a'bowin' an' a'swayin'

an' the puffs on the stem
with vi an' with vim
was a'breezin' an' a'sneezin'

an' the trash in the lane
the much of a pain
was a'runnin' an' a'flyin'

an' the girl of the sun
with top on the run
was a'yellin' an' a'jigglin'

an' the trees in a row
with bangs on the blow
was a'snigglin' an' a'gigglin'

හ○ශ

Seasonal Symphony

A soft euphony of undertoning purling and rustling-demuring
scored the symphony of eve.

Orchestra members gently whispered and brushed
against one another as they tuned.

Ascending atop the mound with gust-baton,
maestro dipped and bowed.

Concert vituosos twirled in wild applause
in lush-darkened, diamond-glimmered hall.

Without overture, the orchestra burst forth *accelerando,*
rocking back and forth, waving and bobbing, *furioso,*
frantically fanning and nodding, breathtakingly
performing "the rustling silk rhapsody," *fortissimo,*
then, gradually, began swaying *adagio,* and eased
into the strain, "jillions upon jillions of tiny bubbles
popping on a screen," *pianissimo...intimo...*
With faintest wave of baton, a wind chime tinkled *giocoso,*
ear-teasing, in the distance,

while wheeling windmills, spinning pinwheels,
and swiveling weather vane continued
whirling wild exuberant *bravos.*

April '97

      I strolled through
Bluegrassland's morning-cool
along deserted,
slow-winding, back road.

      Days, warm and summery
had wed freezing nights,
and borne budding trees,
and perked bulbed flowers,
and raised early gardens--all nipped in their might.
Struggling, new beginnings
sighed in refractory
amid leftover browns and wintry grays
unable to mate with spring.

      In a curve of the road,
trickled-down stream
ran cross-wise in a gully,
and stepped around stones,
and through channel beneath.

 Wild greening fields,
strewn with straw-brown tufts
and volunteer trees, lounged
on both sides of morn-sunned road,
fenced by rusting barbed wire.

      Trees stood
on rolling knolls,
waving shyly from three heights--
background trees,
tall, bare gray,
held spreading branches
and branchlets toward sky,
tops sprayed in arcs
like fancy fans church ladies wave.
Mid-stood trees
wore beautiful, delicate, white

--sometimes pink--blossoms,
and flared outward
like crippled umbrellas.
And shortest trees,
groomed to be front and center,
decked themselves in spring-green.

        Terrain hiked
downward into a gulch
in left pasture--where other fan trees
stretched their arms and fingers above--
then climbed back up again.
A few splotchy white cows,
and a calf or two, walked
languidly toward the fence,
chewing, and quietly watching.
And mid-field, alone, glowered
a *wicked* thorn tree,
inch-spikes, intervaled two inches apart,
on staunch guard along twisty branches
gnarling downward,
and snaking meanly
around its beleaguered trunk.

        Sparse cedars stood
along fence lines;
and green bushes, where
honeysuckle blossoms would appear,
wrestled with vibrant vines,
frost-murdered weeds,
and dew-bent sapling leaves.

        Air sang alive
in every tone and voice--
piercing trilling,
raspy jabbering,
lovely twittering,
sta-sta-stuttering,
and quickly-drilled chattering,
sounds of international staccato:

jah-ho-be/jah-ho-be/jah-ho-be jah
jewi jewi jewi
weejah-weejah/weejah-weejah
meitmeitmeitmeit
chee-me chee-me chee-me
qwiqwiqwi-ee,qwiqwiqwi-ee
oo cheche-ah, oo cheche-ah
jitjitjitjitjit, jitjitjitjitjit
ge-ah! ge-ah! ge-ah! ge-ah!
meip meip chchchchee, meip meip chchchchee
whitwhitwhit je-ahh!
wurple heep, wurple heep, wurple heep
kilkilkilkilkilllll
etwah-ee etwah-ee etwah-ee.

Ahead, across the road,
lulled a stocky herd of cows
--bulls--
stepping and moving in tandem
with a ponderous, black leader,
who began galloping
--so did his retinue--
when he glimpsed me approaching.
My eyes nervously swept
the four thin strands of barbed wire...
When he had made
the ground rumble, and had
ca-plocked enough, he made
a wide turn,
--so did they, like migrating flock--
earth thundering,
and ran back...made another wide
turn, and thundered back--and forth
--Males--
until I passed.

Further on, tree-line
and thick bramble huddled
together,
hiding fields from the road.

        Meanwhile, left, fields
continued lounging and meandering
tranquilly--with high, dry,
yellow grasses standing around
in the meadow,
kissing up to a scum pond--
and hosting lonely, solitary
oak, cedar, ash, and beech,
as well as clumps of locusts,
of which,
four more wicked thorn trees
stood and watched me.

ଚ୍ଚX୍ଚ

Walk

In the sky, the sun burst yellow,
surging rays in waves of light swing,
shafting down the glitz on glare sprees,
shimmer-glint as glimmered rain beads.

Tops of trees were doused with saffron;
drizzling drops of beam through branches;
dripping light among the leaf shade,
freckled green with gold-spritz sun weave.

Eye-squint gleam streamed past the fences;
washing citron over landscape;
spraying sheen on turf green carpet,
plush and thick as sable brushes.

Here and there clinked chimes; were birdbaths,
garden huts and rad gazebos;
stain-glass butterflies on stigma;
bumble bees deep-kneed in pollen.

Robins, hummingbirds, and finches,
sang and soared and hovered sprightly,
'round strung feeders, vanes, and benches
placed near shrubs, and plants and bushes.

From the cottage clenched in ivy,
stirred a stroller quietly thinking.

Blossoms bloomed among the gardens;
staking high the green sword sepals
holding limp the soft pink dresses
of the glads with speckled edges.

Hollyhocks with crimson petals
bled on spikes in wide corollas,
jutting yellow, tongue-clung pollen
for the kisses of the bombus.

Daffodils sipped, cup-and-saucer,
on green stems, in creamy lemon,
puddingly cups of butterscotch,
custard pie and French vanilla.

Flames of orange tongued silken purple
soft-wave iris scarves unfurling
supple folds of ruffled fringes,
from tall-spiring, smooth green vases.

To his stroll, the scen'ry motioned;
lilies nodded, ragweed wavered.
Near the pond, swayed reeds and rushes;
pushed beyond, bowed thirsty weed grass.

From the ground grew scorn, came thistle,
bane of fields and branded noxious;
ribwort leaf, the scourge of grasses
strove in tandem with the fescue.

Here seductive, here undaunted,
trefoil vied among the hostas;
there wild rooted, lone they flourished,
there ruled briefly...reigning lawn kings.

From their presence, he felt comfort,
comfort of unhailed existence;
in their refuge, he sensed kindness,
of defiant, winning spurgeweed;

of the shunned, the purple-berried--
purple-berried, red-vein root stalk,
soon to be the mulch of mowers,
it Crayola'd strong as tulips.

Purposely, he kindred soft-spoke,
to the fallen, rear, wood step rail,
broken stealth by toadstool quietness,
while it stood secure and steadfast.

Maiming wood, umbrellas scalloped;
mushroom caps staked root, unyielding;
through the steps, the fungus burrowed;
shoved its down-shoot through the punctures;
pushed its will above the pulped wood...
left it lying cracked and open.

There he saw wood, soft and pulpy,
on the lawn, lie cracked and open.

To the pebbled, tan-white step stones,
leading to a gritty foot path,
stepped the stroller in reflection--
stinging nettle near and skulking.

Shadow gray-laid, in a moment;
from above, a cloudburst opened.
Rain, gent-drizzling warmth and coolness,
kept him in it like a mallard,

Eyes and ears and sense wide open
listening to the quiet rain murmur,
gurgling low like oil and wet pain,
as it gently flowed the rock slopes.

Then as swiftly, grayness moved on;
just as swiftly then the sun shone.
Tint-shades lasered from the stone-glaze
with parades of sprays and pompons,

shoots with sprigs, and floret clusters;
trimming walks with bouquet fragrance:
rose-filled thick with ambush colors
like black blood and velvet salmon--

or the twin-starred, pendant lilac,
or viburnum popcorn layers.

On the path, the zinnias rainbowed;
fuchsias pinked and snowballs ice-creamed,
till the wet high-beamed the colors,
blinding him, and he deflected.

Streaming, yellow sunshine sprayed him;
strong and yellow like a pee stream;
it felt stinging—scathing—callous,
as it burned away his cover.

Hastening through the picket gateway,
past the honeysuckle hedges,
toward the woods' shade outer edges,
locking on the leaved-topped sanctum,

he tripped over broken half shells--
split and dried out, shells of hick'ry,
looking up with hollow-eye stares
so invasive, so self-stripping.

Moss-thin carpet felt his crossing--
carpet staked with green-tree shadow,
whisper-still as hide-seek quietness,
which precedes a fierce wind's lashing.

Toward a sturdy oak he staggered,
gripped the bulk of grainy roughness;
turned and brushed the tactless stinging;
muffled back the threatening whimper,
while the deaden-daiquiris lowered him,
numb and slow against the tree trunk.

Letting go, he fumbled spacey;
fractured thoughts, and ran within them;
found his way out through the anguish;
tried to suckle some protection,
in the fetal curved position
of his mind, betrayed and fearful.

In his hand, he traced its promise;
sleep and void was what he wanted.
He gazed at the green above him,
saw the leaves move, heard its wind song;
felt the rev that seized his body;

branched his mind and flowed within it;
found his way out through the thicket;
tore at all the brush and bramble;
broke away into the sun slit;
scurried back along the gray crest;
grabbed a vine while pain-deciding...

(as the woods grew nestled thickly
on dark floors of twigs and nut hulks,
seeds, the acorn caps and heal roots,
twisted wild with vines and saplings,
lichen bark and jungle frond'd ferns.

Squirrel jumps rustled leaf to limb-leap;
canopied birds sang soothing Qual.
Breeze pursued the tall red cedars,
hung with blue-hued berry clusters.

Wild blackberries bulged chin juicy
on thick bushes, lush and spiny)
...if he would...or reconsider...
trace his steps...or start a dirge march...

Dread-soaked clouds, dark and descending,
drenched his soul in midnight blackness,
raining rash-filled, mind-screw whispers,
rasped through fiendish-howled illusions.

Tasting tears, he bayed in drunk angst,
bellowing torn and shudder-wracked
to the still, white flow'ring dogwoods
breathing softly in the hushed woods.

When Darkness Came

In whilom time before the seen world was...
before eves fell and mornings broke
upon premier dawn of the dark spheroid,
and jagged, fallow-lain crust flooded white...
was love stone-set, age-old DNAed
of constancy and endurance sinew,
sustained-lifed by Adonai, the Beginning;
mirrored in flawless matrices of order—
criteria of harmony, and
law:
> wisdom Adonai possessed,
> and knew must be embraced
> to circumvent catastrophe
> he knew existed.
...therefore, in
theorem proof vernacular,
law is love.

From ages extinguished as fading light
of last-life, burned out clockwork stars,
and now, as dusk replenishes dark,
Adonai, incomprehensible
as no origin and no ending,
did not exist inertia-throned
in an ethereal dome... When there
was no unknown nor known,
there was the Son the Word,
pre-existent and onbeing.

Before primeval antiquity yawned,
before primordial null met the edge
of earthlight, Adonai, and the Son,
in concert with the Spiritual Comforter—
Time-Continuum before light convened--
collaboratively spangled galactic voids;
the Word vocalizing synergic conceptions
as worlds and beings and ministering spirits
sprang by uttering of deific vision.

Beings inhabited magnificent joy-spreed worlds,
as light-journeys, on a glass-seemed globe,
celestial attendants flourished, pulsing
at the nucleus of the luminous city
of Adonai, peering over his shoulder
awe-dazed, catching volleyed directives
and whirling back fulfilled commands.
Dynastic courtiers of the universal palace,
they were revered and admired.
They--were angels of God:

of elect-intelligence,
festooned with wings, speed, versatility
and strength; ability to leave Adonai's
presence and be on another world at cosmic
velocity; power to alter form;
to render pending, rendered.

...Enshrouded, and ancient as swirling vapors,
the invisible world only
is see-witness to the exhaustive wardrobe
of unfathomable abilities and
cloaking powers adorning seraphim
and cherubim nobility.

Pronounced as the tinseled profusion
of clustered, whorl-winding skylights
which chandelier the circuitous canopy,
their corps was careered with crown ops
diverse and distinctive.

Master elite,
was their great over-leader, Lucifer;
passionately loved, honored;
perhaps first and oldest of their kind;
the most exquisite, most extraordinary;
peerless in rank and power;
conversant in matters of the realm.

Rival of aurora-radiant light break,
he attentioned beside the Almighty
when myriad worlds assembled,

veiling Adonai with his great wingspread,
an epaulet of splendor.

In shimmering worlds,
awash with wonder and accord,
All breathed peace.

None were abused nor misused--
wholly in consequence of supreme
interplanetary decrees, generating
tranquil stasis, and the essence
of macrocosmic contentment.

And All loved Adonai.

And he desired their love,
giving them all the will to love him
or not to love him. That was his gift.
Thus was his love, the marrow
of his law.

...Irrespective of light-bred knowledge
discovered from core to outer-sphere,
the apparent world can access no annals
citing the expanse of unblemished reign
of peace and serenity which existed in
quondam infinity--whether ages
or eras, millenniums or eons.

But somewhere in the hidden midst of times,
the mind of one began to hatch
strange thoughts, to discern
that he,
the beautiful, the renown,
was increasingly malcontent
being first in his ranks,
and coveted being fourth member
of the exalted Council of Three.

At some breath-catch moment
during the time-elapse of ages,

he began questioning why
he did not have equal place
with powers that are.

Did he not stand nearest Adonai.
Did he not have command of legions.
Was he not esteemed of worlds.

In flashes of self-adoration,
he was lifted up by his beauty,
he,
the magnificence, the light.

Blinded by his own facula brilliance,
he began to see no variance
between himself and
the one enthroned among stars.
In his fantasies
of exaltation and grandeur,
no one else presented resplendence
worthy of his aspiration
—or envy.

In stolen moments of petulance,
he grew desires to be god-like, and
to have the homage of other beings.

Though breeding delicious reverie
hard-pulsing his reins,
had he spliced equipoise
to reason through disparate thoughts
of aspiring to be as Adonai;
to delve into his speculative notions,
his resolve would have eclipsed
the cresting of night.

Lucifer, created personage,
chose to envision equality
with the Creator,
obsessing in conjecture of how
this ascendancy might be attainable.

On a palette of pureness, of naiveté
and fidelity, where his thoughts now
collided, his bile began to seep.

Through intimacies of camaraderie,
of groupthink and executions,
stifled stirrings seeped and diffused,
as Holies inhaled incongruence.

Omniscient, and acutely cognizant
of the concatenation of events
transpiring in a transparent
corner of the empire,
the Council suffered
anguish unknown in the known
or unknown world.
They had architected reason
and will in all.
All built-in tranquility and risk
now quavered, pulsing
portentous under-currents.

Adonai, foreseer of creeping midnight,
sought the sun shafts of dialogue,
but Lucifer, he
the wisdomed, the sum of Gifted,
had exchanged envy
for entitlement and jealousy.
As surely as the sequestered sessions
he could not attend,
he would have allegiance,
and, parity with Adonai.

Submerged in deeply nested cunning
and stealth, he custom-crafted stratagem
to ambush the notions of his comrades.

Debuting subterfuge hidden as night within,
while unveiled in high sight of day,
he counsel-questioned
among his kin

why consummate glory and deference
were not due him,
sublime, star-cut luminary,
high noble of the empire.

As moons cycled, and disquiet caressed the calm air,
every inhabitant of the universe
became aware of what was supervening
with the beloved Lucifer,
he
the admired, the venerable,
and were troubled.

The Supreme Three, quintessence of reason,
released revisited communiqués
re-saying parameters and powers,
reviewing the wisdom of omniscient delegation;
reiterating the dynamics of love,
law, and peace.

Lucifer, he
the anointed, the loftily appointed,
instead fantasized that his high
honor and position were due
to his own phenom and worthiness,
and continued with unvoiced desire
to be supreme,
and, in resentment.

Why should he not be honored?
He, Lucifer, shadow-walked
by hierarchies of select intels
who breathed in, after he exhaled?
He, locus witcher, imbibing enabling license
infiltrating their God-forged core?

Chameleon ever garbed in new guise,
Lucifer evoked dichotomy
from the wind and sky,
impugning the Council,
politicizing from both sides
of his beauteous mouth.

Camouflaging with precise perfidy
his own ambitions,
he reinvented them as those of angels.
Angelkind, fertile tabula rasa,
were inoculated by his novel acuity.

Adonai, citadel of actuating love,
endeavored to dissuade
darling, subversive Lucifer,
giving him opportunity to realize
his thinking was fallacious chaff,
and to repose in the respite of clemency.

Unable to sublimate intervals
of intrusive introspection, amid
ambition to be god,
Lucifer muzzled qualm and colors
and pushed aside reconciliation.

Within perpetuity, both light and dark,
this precipitous decision
broadsided reality,
and three-sixty'd the universe.

Determinedly moving forward,
like interlocking gears
of a first-tick timepiece
wound with springs of straining power-lust,
of tightening enmity,
his true purposes surged.
Game-changing,
he petitioned proselytes
to consign allegiance to him,
self-groomed power broker,
the righter of egregious inequities;
pretender pro tem.

Millions of winged beings breast-saluted...
and defected to Lucifer.

As the morphing order grappled
and molted their innocence, Lucifer,

greedy to retain all clan
of his newly formed crest, unpeeled
fraternity and slid into impeccable treachery,
as he caringly applied fake poultices to
their swelling trepidation, and
deftly cauterized their exuding doubts;
sealing every way of any return to Adonai;
they now,
forfeiters of royal place and unceasing existence.

...*They* were the *first* casualties of darkness...

...millions upon millions and millions
of doting devotees--actuated by
adulation of Lucifer.
And Lucifer?...
the musical, the pied piper of artifice,
the consummate opportunist?
...actuated by egocentricity,
he,
the contender to godhood, aspirant
to eminent rule...The progenitor of chaos.

Millions more special class corps
rallied to Adonai.

The kingdom, surreal, stood edgy.

Adonai, decision-think advocate,
bestorer of will, did not annihilate,
did not impede, did not intervene.
He foreknew this possibility
when brainchilding children of will.
Now, one of his children
was exercising that will.

Unprecedented, and dark-swelling
on the uni-world horizon, the dilemma
rendered it imperative that
all dispel prevailing haze
and peer the darkness of Lucifer's full intent—
and encompassing consequences.

Bathed in beaucoup acclaim and celebrity,
Lucifer's spurious influence
had serpentined galactic oceans,
breaching the thinking of some from afar,
emotionally challenging the norm,
and posturing abeyant sympathy.

Not vested with thought-read faculties,
neither angels nor world inhabitants
omosed that Lucifer,
honored stakeholder of the realm,
had resolutely,
and irrevocably severed affiliation,
was jockeying for the loftiest pinnacle;
would revoke realm-stemmed precepts,
establish a reign of half-truths,
and eventually, of tyranny.

Himself the unseen seer, sheathed
beside the moving minutes, Adonai
knew created beings could not fine-focus
a millenniums-marooned world reeling
from recalcitrant actions just set in motion.

Nor did any understand that existence
outside interplanetary decrees
of Adonai would become degenerate life.
These existential actualities
required incontrovertible proof.

While the universe teetered,
while the spun top pivoted,
Adonai permitted Lucifer to proceed carte blanche
with his pandemic domino topple,
that mutational virulence and depravity,
which his deviation from universal law
would eventually spawn,
would be unveiled to all who were
and were to come.[1]

---

[1] E.G. White, *Patriarchs and Prophets*, Pacific Press Publishing Association;
1958, p. 41-42.

...Revealed-world universities and museums
contain no scrolls, no tablets of clay
documenting the interminable continuum
Adonai permitted Lucifer
to vilify him and to grow hostilities.

But as events clocked, Lucifer's rebellion
ripened to open revolt.

Counter and counter-countering, the countdown ratcheted...

... And there was war in heaven:

alien acts of aggression...
metamorphosing former cohorts
of brotherhood and kinship,
of supernatural strength and power
into opposing combatants with capability
to inflict injury and pandemonium
the magnitude of apparent-world
weaponry.

Adonai, awesome impetus who
kindled constellations, breath-fused
biosphere, teemed undarkened seas,
was more than apt
to *pronounce* the faction out of
existence—and unsparingly quash
the insurrection.
Whether he expeditiously throttled,
or even when war-thrust,
extended the olive branch,
is unknown to the perceived world.

Jeweled crown amid the vast arena
of a sweeping world,
the royal province, sprawling terrestrial beauty,
unrolled regions-stretched terrain
from which rebels launched, retreated and ranged.

Terrene archives stow no secrets
of classified military strategies,

or scripts of skirmishes,
or the length Adonai tolerated
the battling battalions.

But, at his own providential hand wave,
Adonai commanded the assault
to cast Lucifer and his cabal
from the imperial capital-planet
of transparent-gold boulevards
under-bedding rainbow-reflecting gems;
from the dazzling, gilt-hued megalopolis
of palatial gardens
and magnificent palaces.

...Known-world scholars possess no data
documenting the actual incident
resulting in the exile of the warring hopefuls.
Given their super might
and envisioned stakes,
it may have been necessary
to oust Lucifer and his insurgents
from the planet with extreme force;
his expulsion executed
through incomprehensible dynamisms
of energy physiced by beings,
unachievable in the physical world.
It may have been that the same result
as that achieved by known-world
aeronautical geniuses had to be
accomplished--to eject him clear
of the force of gravitational pull.

Whatever the catalytic particulars
of his catapultic expulsion...
Lucifer fell from heaven as lightning;
as a streaking meteor...
he,
the light, the brilliant star.

And all the universe was somber. Was changed...

...Archeologists of the defined world,
however learned and field-accomplished,
will never unearth the capital
where the millions set up government,
one which that day strangle-fed god-thirst gnawing;
one which scarf-devoured platform and promise;
a government of failures and railings,
of plots and counter-betrayals;
where peace dissolved;
where regret numb-sat among ashes,
where triumph, stuttering, sought to be salvaged.

In Adonai's royal city, subdued and sorrowed,
the unparalleled supervention,
had routed and vaulted Lucifer,
but not cherry-picked issues,
nor seeds of a no-rules utopia
promised by a would-be ruler,
and littered upon the perspective
of a now perplexed universe.

In a decision designed to forever
mute inference of transcendent
existence, goodness and peace,
apart from the tenets of goodness
and the Giver, Adonai would not
eradicate the rebels until all createddom
witnessed the unfettered progression
of God-free consciousness and will. [2]

In pre-times, globevolutions before--
contingency for deliverance from darkness,
for restoration of light,
was drafted by the sagacious Three,
sourced within a timetable,
in the event creatures of will
made the unthinkable choice.

And so, from cyclical twilights
evanesced into yesternights,

[2] E.G. White, *Patriarchs and Prophets*, Pacific Press Publishing Association;
1958, p. 41-42.

seasons passed, life continued,
forever altered, with less sense of
peace and inner quietude among
all beings, and a great sense of
loss and grief.

Beings continued to inhabit their
magnificent planets and to assemble in
the great city to worship. Angels continued
to bustle-stir throughout the buoyant universe.
The Council continued to conceptualize,
and bright-design new worlds.

...The most powerful space-beamed
telescopes of the discernible world
cannot detect whether Adonai duplicated
all living worlds, or whether
they are each diverse,
with distinct color schemes,
or plant systems, or primary life;
whether all have stars or moons or suns
or other planetary bodies.
Each living world-system was spoken
into existence in seven rotations.
The inhabitants of each come together
at dusk's kneel on each seventh eve
to gather in the great city of angels,
to worship in gratitude before
the Creator.

...And, after the master genesis
of an inchoate orb, sidereal year
unknown to the seeable world,
the Council implemented the perfecting
of a living world which was third planet
from its sun.

And Lucifer and his millions,
ever fresh from council
to continue battle,
to fly afresh in the face of Adonai,
to defame

and dishonor,
to gain ascendancy,
flew from their rock, as it were,
like disturbed bats from a cave,
and in synchronicity,
hurtled toward the planet...
their journeying resonating through
times, past archived epochs, to dawns
that have yet to rekindle day.

...And, the evening and the morning
were the first sunrise of an impending
second daybreak of darkness.

ಐಂಬ
2
ಐಂಬ

Dusty Album On the Back Shelf

We Do Not Have Roaches

We do not have roaches.
The *landlord* says we do not have roaches.

When we sleepily reach for toothbrushes every morning,
        it is not a *roach* that outruns
                the smack of our hands
                        down through the basin drain.

There are no roaches *here.*
        Those are not roaches that form a living floor
                and run helter-skelter at night
    whenever we flick
        on the kitchen light.

No roaches *live* here.
        When we have company,
        and the heater is turned high,
        those are not roaches that
                swarm out of the wood
                        and leap from the walls
                                like dive bombers.

Those are not roaches that our friends keep watching
        from the corners of their eyes,
                and shake
                        from their coats
                                before they leave.

We *have* no roaches.
The *landlord* says we have none.

-old photograph of apartment in Santa Barbara around 1968

Land Where My Fathers Died
(on knee)

of thee I sing
off-key

of the free and the brave
unfree

let freedom ring
justly

sweet land of libber
tea

-national portrait (somewhere in the 70's)

☙❦

Home

America...America,
I somehow love
you so,
but I always yearn to know
the earth place I might sow,
if you hadn't dropped-swapped your hoe
to exploit my black body so.

-view from a window left open in my country - 1979

The Man

He's the only man
I've ever met,
who can talk faster than I can,
who can out-think me,
who can come up with
quicker, better defenses—
who can cause me
to do things for
him
that I said--
        unequivocally--
        he'd do--or consequences;
He's the only man
I know
who's barely four.

*-picture of "an old man who has been here before" (Nigerian friend's description) -
1979*

ଶ୦ଓଷ

That Time

It was the time
my first baby, wren-small, came...
when I stood life-dazed before a judge,
representing myself in divorce...

The time
I took my life from freeze-frame,
attending college by mental nudge,
setting my life on a "take-two" course...

It was the time
I was at the border of thirty,
...but it was the first time I grew.

-glimpse of 1975-77

Accolades--From the Down Side

He appears an unlikely candidate
to be where he is--
sitting there with too-high trouser legs,
exposing same-socks
day after day,
and shoes I would have
long discarded,
or saved for slumming at home;
wearing a thin, high-neck sweater
with creases of both sleeves
iron-hit in two separate places,
pushed past his wrists,
revealing muscled arms and hands;
      his hair, jagged-parted
         and nonchalantly smoothed,
    highlighting graying temples.

And, when he looks down
at his book as he speaks,
his face catches the shadow
and has an unshaven look
-reminiscent of some old sea hand...

And, as I survey him,
I wonder how he came to be here--
this Learned Professor, in this
Prestigious University
lecturing about Williams, and Eliot,
Pound, the Dadaists, "The Waste Land,"
dominant feet...
about Everyone and Everything
I've never heard of,
with so
much Insight,
and so much Knowledge,
and is so Well-Versed,
and is
such a Literary Heavy,
that he is
a *screaming* bore...

-frame from American Lit Class, USC - Mar 1979

Riddle

Who are you that shake the head at South Africa?...
Who are you that speak against denying human rights?...
Who are you that discuss the evils of apartheid?...
Who are you that champion the rights of *other* downtrodden
peoples?...
Who are you that think your stance has always been on the side of
right?...
Who are you that think you always wear the white hat?...

-blurred perspective- 1981

ဆာ၄၃

Synonyms

a-p-a-r-t-h-e-i-d   -Afrikaans
s-e-g-r-e-g-a-t-i-o-n   -American English

~~change~~
sing a new song

-superimposed time images – 1981

Report Card--Needs Improvement

Five years ago,
        my life--already Richter-shaky--
completely collapsed;
I and the man
I'd vowed to gray with,
were no longer part of each other..
after months that heaved and swayed,
his baby came...

...The upheaval
        of torn-turned pages is past,
and I made it through with less pain
than I'd imagined...

Returning to halls and books,
I embraced new people,
One in particular...
        (I never thought I'd come to the end of *that...*)
...all is behind now,
and here in this fifth calendar,
I'm experiencing the burnout
of being a single mother and a student
 (I must finish...I must finish...).

With no deeper
spiritual growth
than before,
in economic chaos,
with bungee-cording weight,
running in place,
        and contemplating marriage
to a man I don't even know.

-close-up - Mar 1980

Reverberations

Oh! HAVE MERCY!

Why doesn't she shut UP?!
       Doesn't she know how much
       she bugs me?

Doesn't she get tired of talking
about the
same thing
over and over?

Doesn't she
get tired of yakking
about what I didn't do
every time
she comes home?

When I have kids, I'll
never harp on and on
like that...

   ...What's that you
   said to me, Boy?--
   ...What do you mean,
   I BUGS you?!

-in two different places – 1980

Suicide

I never think about her
        because...
I don't want to;
and when I do,
        I quickly think of something else.

I see her pictures,
        but
I spend no time studying them.
I look at them, and then
        find something else to gaze upon.

I don't think about
our beginnings--about how close we never were.

I speak superficially of her
        because...
I have to.

I don't want to ever miss her...
and I won't allow
the frenzy of tears,
and anguish,
and rage,
to occur very often.

-photo in low light, Feb 15,1977

My Usetobe

Love is such a fragile emotion
flown on the whimsy wings of
some conceptualized bird,

(whose course is rarely delineated,
whose destination, barely discernible),
who never lights where intended—

On approaching its place of landing,
the courier of love is deflected—
its hue—strange, its plume—scanty,
its refrain —unrecognizable...

For love's song, sang ever so ardently,
may never be heard in the hearer's heart,
if it were awaiting love...in another key.

Of the many, endless renditions of love—
if none were translatable into the receiver's tongue,
it is as though the lover never loved.

And so to you, who never believed I ever loved you,
who felt disillusioned, rejected—even betrayed,
because I was not loving you the way you needed to be loved,

--I cry softly as I say, I'm sorry,
       I didn't have the code,
       I didn't know the cipher,
       I didn't possess the key,
       I didn't know there was another way,
               my usetobe.

-backwards glance – undated

Before Reality

-Little girls are so sweet, she says.
-I can't stand little girls, I say.

-They always look so dainty all dressed up, she continues.
-They look prissy, I correct her--prissy.

-Don't you just love to see them in pretty, sheer dresses, little fancy underpants, fluffy crinoline slips, cute little ruffled socks, little delicate, lacy gloves...satiny ribbons? she rambles on.
-I am not a friend to ruffles or bows, satin or fluff, I pointedly inform her.

-It's always so much fun to style little girls' hair, she floats dreamily on.
-It is not fun to be entangled in a mass of hair with a fidgety, whimpering little girl, I block.

-Girls acquire verbal proficiency skills much earlier than boys, she loads.
-Little girls *always* talk too much, I return her serve.

-They mature faster than boys too, she adds for flavor.
-They *are* too grown, I agree.

-Girls are good to have around--someone to talk to, to be close to, she goes into high gear.
-Mother/daughter relationships are clouded and complex at best, I grate.

-Sugar and spice, and everything nice, she recites.
-I'm a boy-mommy! I say too loudly. My first one was a boy; he wears rough-dried clothes, and *has* no hair! I was meant to mother *boys*!

-What girl's name have you picked out? she plods blithely on.
-I'm not having a girl! I snap. He'll be named after his father!

-Oh, I hope you do have a girl, she insists.
-I won't! I assure her.

-collective collage before daughter's birth -1983

Just Me

Edie —
I take this name in marriage
knowing I have none other;

Having expectantly exchanged
the surname of my father;
I now enlightened return the name
of my husband.

Once, self was defined by either or.
Now, time-grown, I'm neither nor.
I am just...Edie
to have and to hold.

-solitary image, circa 1979

ഇരുൽ

Roots

Have a sweet potato and butter--
-I don't want *that*.

Well, here, eat some corn bread and greens--
-Ugh--no! *That* won't get it.

-You know what I really want, Ma?
Some lasagna, or some enchiladas--
Oh, I know, what's that stuff in shells--
manicotti? yeah. And some "jerk" chicken,
uh huh. How 'bout some juevos rancheros?
Make mine with shredded beef and melted
cheese, topped off with a salad.
How that sound?

You know wha'chu kin do?--take yo' California-bred
palate, and go find yoself some Arugula and radicchio,
while these butter beans and collards get ate.

-dinner scene in Kentucky - Dec 1993

Post Love

Inside my treasure drawer
are priceless tokens...of no pecuniary value...

...**A** miniature bell,
the span of two thimbles,
with an eyelet crown;
of poor metal,
producing a clear tingling sound;
the outside, silvery-gray and tarnished,
the underside, a green cast
with tiny, pin-spots of rust;
the rim, slightly bent--
effecting an oval cant...

A long red ribbon was threaded
through the crown
for her to hold and summon me
as she wasted away.
The sharp clarity of the tiny bell
as she rang--and rang,
nearly drove me mad,
and caused me to curse the day
I'd given it to her.
I swore it'd be the first thing
I'd get rid of
when she surrendered life...

...**A** pair of ungainly black shoes,
graceless, lace-up shoes,
with five eyelets
and dirty, felt-lined tongues;
with thick, three-layer soles
so flat and stiff,
they "smack" against the floor...
ugly, deformed-looking
--embarrassing--shoes,
which confusingly look
neither like a left, nor a right;

the soles, so piteously scraped,
they're worn down in patches
through the second layer of leather--
the right one, more harshly.

Inside the small child's shoe
is printed *Tarso Pronator*...
--beautiful shoes--
which straightened his uncooperative, twisted foot.

-treasured heirlooms (1986) and (1978)

ಹಿ೧೮

Heart

Boy of seven,
please live on,
because my heart
would be so quiet
if you were gone.

Please...live to eight.

Boy of mine,
near end of nine,
you've made my heart
fall again.

Please...live to ten.

-special photos, heart failure, 1982 and '84

Not Forgotten

The headlights,
as they came 'round Lookout Mountain,
glimmered against the darkened wall
like stars.
Though miles away,
she could see them
from her upstairs window.

In the next room,
her brother listened to music
on an antiquated, upright radio.
Downstairs, one sister was banging
on the untuned piano,
and the other--nowhere to be seen.
The youngest was jabbering, unminded,
in the high chair.
From the common yard
of brick row houses,
children's voices--laughing, shrieking, teasing--
filtered up to the window.

Watching the diamonds travel
up and down the incline
made her ache--
a pain of envying things unknown;
of desperately wanting something different,
envying unknown people--
going to, coming from, unknown places,
their lives, she envisioned,
better than her own--
the food they ate - more filling,
the clothes they wore - more becoming.

She watched each headlight
flicker in and out
and disappear, and reappear,
and ached because they were free
to go and come.

She determined, in time,
she would be free--
free of McCallie Homes,
free of the stagnancy of the town,
free of being poor and stymied.

Look at the headlights, and remember
she commanded herself,
and promise that when things have changed,
you will never forget.

-picture of a childhood memory, Chattanooga, circa 1960

ഽറ

Advice to a Twelve-Year Old

Quit, with your exclusive clubs
and relationships that exclude
and leave some on the outside
knocking and so alone.

You know the feel of rejection--
use that non-acceptance
to sharpen your own sensitivity
and invite others under your wingspan.

Expand yourself, your circle,
to include
the old, the very young,
the embarrassing,
the ones with missing or imperfect parts,
the zit-faced,
the ugly,
the klutz, the dweeb that no one wants around,
the non-talented,
the chubby, the bean pole,
the have-nothings,
the pesky,
those who stink,
and the quietly-lonely.

-cropped photo of a microcosm - 1995

Interruption

Soaking up sun
        through a window's warmth--
        leisurely savoring a book
        like simmered stew,

Awareness is arrested--
        windows are rattling,
        storm door clattering,
        lace curtains shimmy over panes.

Leaves scuttle swiftly 'cross the lawn--
        sky is dark'ning,
        rain, pa-tinging.

Run relay between raindrops—
        wash is wind-whipped on lines...
        the fury is lashing,
        the torrent, sheeting.

As an encore,
        rush out,
        roll up car windows,
        race back--wringing wet.

The back door bangs open,
        rain bullets the floor;
        scramble for a mop,
        batten-ram the door.

Sprint spryly for firewood,
        wild weather is rolling in...
        then... ol' arbitrary orb--
        out somersaults sun again.

-scene one lazy spring afternoon - Apr 1990

Official

'Bout time...

From the moment the vessel what's-its-name disgorged Africans in Jamestown settlement, in word, in print, and in official records, assault and assassination began:

✓picaninny
✓darkie
✓spook
✓coon
✓sambo
✓ape, "the missing link"
✓spade
✓---NIGGA
anything...anything but...and continued:

✓boy, gal
✓uncle
✓auntie
✓mammy
✓colored [check-this-box-if-you-are begins]
✓Moor (literary-all-inclusive-mystique-mistakenly-synonymous-with-black-Africa-black)
✓jungle bunny
✓neegra (mouthed-by-the-supposed-polite-who-just-couldn't-bring-himself-to-"dignify"-me-with-negro)
✓ Negro [check-this-box-if-you-are changes and continues]
✓Afro-American [tentative-"militant"-appeaser-check-this-box-if-you-are]
✓Black [35-year-run-check-this-box-if-you-are]

...Was it by use in a speech, a poem, a plea, presidential proclamation, political ratification, or people's popular poll that our now-name was nominated, ruminated, and our ethnic status came to be reclassified and officially declared, Again?

-African American (true-dignity-of-real-significance-actual-designation-as-a-people)

'Bout time...

- *vigil at the statehouse, for about 250 years*

Till Death Do Us Part

Plunging heart, all hope deplete
Quavering arms, in quiet retreat
Emulsing bowels, in risk replete
Floating legs of icy sleet

> ...seismic fears
> ...pendular emotions
> ...paroxysmal thoughts

Vacillating lips, no words complete
Swimming eyes, no stares can meet

> Death throes
> of the union
> between a man
> and a woman.

-taken at the scene of death -1975

ઠ૦ભ

When Love Has More Promise than Love Songs

When love has more promise than love songs,
When smiles have more real than lust,
When lips have more true than guile,
When give has more all than terms,
When talk has more seek than hedge,
When hearts have more vow than rings—
Love will have more close than cry.

-introspective negative, undated

Wordsome

You worry me to no end
    with your incessant talking,
        your hypotheses, your suppositions,
            your reasonings, your proposals,
                your ponderings,
                    your what-can-we-talk-about,
                        your high-pitched voice,
                            your over-exact diction.

I'm thinking.
    I'm trying to *hide* within myself.
        I'm trying to come up with a coup for writers' block.
        I'm fantasizing about your father and me.

"Why can't you hurry up and finish saying what you're saying"?!
    "Will you be *quiet*"?
        "will you just go somewhere"!

I can harshly, impatiently, say all of this to you,
    with sentences machine-gunned in my mind,
        but never will I, with my bullet-tip tongue.

Don't you dare go away. Don't you ever stop talking.
    Don't you ever stop asking me to talk to you,
        or to write you little silly notes,
        or to talk about that dumb cat,
            or to ask about your one pubic hair.
                Don't you ever think I don't want
                    to be bothered with you.
                    Don't you ever stop
                      pestering me.

-clear shot – 1993

LETTER TO MY MOTHER

United States of America
March 5, 1979

My Dear Mother,

I do not know precisely to what place to address you. I have been in another land a long time, and I do not know exactly where I can locate you now. It is my hope that this communication eventually reaches you.

I have long wanted to know you, Mother, but for so many generations, those here had made me ashamed that I was your child. They spoke many things about our homeland...that it was a dark and ignorant place. They told me that I was dark and ignorant, like you. They made me feel ashamed of you, Mother...

This is just a longly-belated search of re-acquaintance, from your daughter, telling you that I wish that I could have known you, and loved you, and been able to speak of you, and, that I would like to be able to see who you truly are, and embrace you...

Mother... Mother--what would my *name* be? *My name*. I have many children now. All of their names were taken away--or borrowed--or invented, not at all what you would have called them. I would revel to hear *my own name, in my own tongue*.

Oh, Mother! I really need to know my first home, the bed of my birth! I need to know of my own beginnings there, so that I can let go of the ones I had here. I want to see my *own* place. I have been in this place so long.

Mother...have you missed me--or the presence of my children... any?..

Mother, when you do meet me, please forgive my shameful ignorance of you; I know that I will embarrass you when I open my knowledgeless mouth.

Since being here, I have undergone so many changes; even my features have been altered. This letter contains a picture of me, Mother. It is my hope that you will still be able to recognize me. Please...Mother ...please, study my face...and tell me where I once belonged.

Lovingly,
Your displaced daughter

-picture-puzzle of Mother – 1979

No

You wonder about me,
        don't you?

Why I won't do this, and why I
won't do that--how come I act
like this, and why I act like that?

I'm your problem, your scourge,
your blight...right?
        ...right.

When I questioned if I had a choice
to come to this land, you said,
"No."

When I begged to be freed,
you said, "No."

When I *longed* to be acculturated
(when there were no ghettos, no
gangs, no drugs to claim me before
I had a say), you said... "No."

When I *craved* an education, would
have done anything to *get* an
education, you said, "No."

When I asked if I could be
allowed an equal entrepreneurial
footing, and social standing, as
any other culture that came to this
land (at least by the third or
fourth generation), you said, "No."

When I implored you meekly, in
fairness, to allow me the same
kinds of jobs you had, to make
the same kind of money you made,
to live the same kind of life-style

you lived, to forge the same
kinds of communities you have,
to invest in the same dream
you dream, you said, "No."

When I asked you if I could be
allowed just plain, human dignity...
you answered, "No."

How about the right to *love* whom
I choose? "NO way."

Make my life where I'd like? "No."

Sip water wherever I'd like? "No."

Sit on the same nasty toilet
you sit on? "No."

If I get some soap so you can't
say I stink--then can I? "No."

What if I burn my hair slick,
so you won't be offended by it?
then? "No."

Alright...I'll struggle, and
overcome all the obstacles
you've set for me, and I'll get an
education anyway... then will
you accept me? "Nope."

What if I fight your wars, and
die for you, so you can offer
freedom to other people?
"No...not really."

If I march peaceable in the
streets for my rights, might I
then have the same freedoms
as you? "Not if we can help it."

If I take you to the highest
court in the land, and win
decisions...? "We'll find
some way to undermine you
back here at home."

If I embrace the tenets of
black militancy... ..."What"?!!

If I take to the street, and
BURN, and fight, and destroy,
will you hear me *then*?!
..."Well...maybe a little,
for a little while...
till the next administration."

You still wondering about me?
You shouldn't.

-old clips – 1980

৪০৫৪

The Same Intolerance

The white face, pushing cart down store aisle,
that snobbishly turns away,
that won't meet my eyes to greet my smile,
much less, force something to say,

Is the same as my black face kinships;
who devour my words on sight,
then intolerantly shape frown-curled lips
with...puh...you sound like you white...

-view outside the mold – 1990

Crop Mentality

Now,
      I am the new crop,
I am the slowly matured harvest of
what you are; of what you seeded---
      disregard of human life, stripping of dignity,
      self-concern and aggrandizement, contempt,
      arrogance, cruelty, humiliation, violation,
      emasculation, disenfranchisement, injustice,
          --hatred.

      I did aspire to be different. I
tried to ripen and mature, despite
what you sowed. I struggled to
produce the "right" crop for well
over 200 years, despite you. But no.

      No, now I am the new crop,
a wild strain, cross pollinated with
frustration, resentment, bitterness
          --rage.

-exposure of social polarization – 1989

ೞೞ

Lil' Brothas and Sistas...

...my message is straight.
It is short, and speaks truth;

You know exactly what I'm talkin' 'bout,
You know exactly who I'm talkin' to;

You might be right--
but you ain't got no excuse.

-another angle of social polarization – 1989

I Suppose It's Prose

It would be wondrous to write poetry--
the kind I grew up with,
which had metrical, rhyming verses
of flawless couplets.

But whenever I try to do it,
roses are red,
violets are blue-
is the only genre I produce.

Stanzas are not consistent,
nor have I grasped anything technical.
Cleverly worded, lyrical phrases
never flow glibly form pen to paper.

Some sigh at knitting sweaters,
or making roofs come out right.
But I sigh when I try to write poetry--
the kind that was lectured about.

Paul Laurence, I love your stuff,
how did you do it--*every time*?
did you have handbooks of versification,
or schemes of poetic lines?

I know--you *studied* hard.
but I'd rather just *write.*
and though I accept that I've neither rhyme nor meter --
　　　I *would* like to ooze--*like Nikki*.

-shot taken at the mill – 1990

Ready--Yet?

There ain' nothing worse
        than unresolved emotions,
        frustrations,
        feelings of insecurity,
        and neuroses,
        roused by one blown-out-of-
        proportion word--OVERWEIGHT.

Mirrors are the enemy:
        "If I just suck in my gut..."
Clothes sizes are the enemy:
        "I was just in a 12/13..."
Memory is the enemy:
        "I used to be sooo skinny..."

But the real enemy is you,
        the one who sleeps with me,
        the lover in my bosom.
        ("Look at yoself sittin' there, Baby!
        you look like a meltin' candle.
        Yo' titties look like they meltin'
        over yo' belly, and yo' belly
        look like it's meltin'
        over yo' thighs
        and yo' thighs--
        Baby, they just meltin'.")

The real enemy is you,
        the one who shares the inner
        sanctum of the bathroom with me.
        ("Baby, if you can't lose it,
        at least tighten it *up*.")

So, like a fool,
        I begin sit ups, curl ups,
        push ups, leg lifts with ankle weights.
        ("Baby, why don't you get up,
        and go runnin'? Go on. I'll let you know
        what happens in the movie.");

Pectoral squeezes and pushes,
thigh presses, bicep curls,
arm lifts, back reaches.
("Baby, [slurp], why don't *you*
just have a small salad"?);

Side twists, overhead reaches,
    steep hill ascents.
    ("Let me have that, Baby.
    you don't need that [burp] second helping.")

Inspections are endured.
    while I'm putting on undies
    after a shower, you do a double-take,
    unsnap something, and squeeze.
    ("Umm, needs a little more work, Baby.")

You press my belly
    to see how tight it feels.
    You watch to see if it bulges
    when I sit down. You pinch the
    adipose tissue on my upper arm
    to see how much has converted into muscle.

And, in the night,
    in the middle of intimacies,
    you take your thumb and your forefinger,
    and you grasp my thigh, and press,
    and I endure, while you check me--
    like some slow-roasting turkey
    you've been waiting for.
    And then, you switch gears and eye-rove.
    (Hey... Baby, yo' neck,
    ain't it gettin' a little loose"?)

-never developed image – 1992

Slipping Away

I want to be able to reach out
and gather us all together,
in my motherly way--
we're all such fragments.

You, big brother--
who's been losing,
and alone, too long--
and my nephew and my niece,
who don't know the rest of us,
and by now, probably don't care.

And my sister--
who needs a major change
to happen
to restore her peace.
Who's given so much
and has so much
and had not enough given.

My baby brother--
with his sweet girls
whom I long to see
who are still mourning their young mother.

And me--
I've had my own adversities,
that none of you know,
as I get older, I realize
that "someday" is never going to come.
And I also think of Daddy--
non-closeness aside
we need to see him--often.

I want us to visit with one another,
to write one another,
to heal and comfort one another,
to rely on one another--is it just a dream?

I don't want us to limp alone--
mother's children, minus one--
I want us to help, to be close.

But the proximities are all wrong,
we're scattered in different cities,
no two bricks upon another.

And meanwhile, while time slips away,
one day at a time,
and as we lost our cousins and uncles and aunts--
      to time
      to distance
      to neglect
our children are losing theirs.

-latest family portrait – 1992

ജാരു

Neogamist's Mad Ride

I don't know
what marriage
is suppose to be--
but it
sho is *hell.*

See, the trick is to embark on
the !!!!!!**SURPRISE**!!!!!! careen through slaloming, screw-
you-too–Hell
while screaming,
LET ME OFFA HERE!!
and come to the other side,
slobberin' and
gigglin' all over yourself,
adrenaline-rushed, memory-bobbed,
dumb-happy as a humping toad, and panting,
Let's do it again.

-good likeness on the convoluting hoop – 1994

Big Difference

Said he wished he had a wife--
when was the last time I cooked?
Told him best to get a life,
mine was already booked.

Complained about the unmade bed
...why he had to iron his shirt.
Told him just to smooth the spread,
...later, would he hit my skirt?...
>   Ask me to work out my life with you,
>   to break cords,
>   to breach doors,
>   to forge love.
>   Ask me to climb astride you,
>   to massage your body,
>   to soothe your mind,
>   to warm your feet,
>   to light your fire.

Said when she'd think of childhood,
she wouldn't recall a sit-down meal.
Told her when she left puerilehood,
she'd be too stuffed to squeal.
>   Ask me to stay home after you're born
>   so you'll feel secure in life,
>   to nurture the flame,
>   to fantail sparks,
>   to hand you the torch.
>   Ask me to stock staples
>   so you'll never be hungry,
>   and blankets and fuel
>   so you'll always be warm.

Love me for what I'm good at.
Accuse me of loving too hard,
of being too protective.
Rework your estimations,
using a truer yardstick:
I'm a nester--
but I'm not domestic.
-sharp picture of life - 1994

You Betta Warn 'Em!

You!...off my desk! what's with you slackers today?!

...I've smacked the top of the wall with *Roget's*, at jabbering,
and flapping of wings, and fanned off things that strayed,
into my computer screen.
      You know I always let you explore the scene.

I don't put out the long guys with stinger quills, who dance
all day at the window sills; or round, fat,
zinger-kings, that push past the front door revving their wings.
      I just let them all have their flings.

If any of you are tub-lounging before my bath, I gently
lift you out of the path of scalding, running
water. And you can scurry down my couch, or you can loiter.
      And no one commences a slaughter.

There are only three offenders (roach-fly-rodent) who are
not welcome-inders, and you already know them. The rest
of you crawl up the wall at leisure, doing whatever will please you.

...And a cousin of yours spins an enormous, white, sac-thing
every fall, by the porch, on the wall, with a web bigger
than my head; and I let it stay, though guests think me unbred.

Some cretins buzz in my ear, or bite in the night, while others
expend energy flicking the lights, batting them annoyingly,
I might add. Do I beak out the Raid, and go mad?!   No.
      I just let you all flow.

But when you sashay into my study
while I'm trying to write—that's where we part ways
and you take a hike.

Tell those guys behind the up-top wall, breaking
my concentration with their nest-building brawl,
they'd better stop it, or I'll spray meanness in the soffit.

And your computer buddies—the could-be gnats?
betta find another screen to party at; betta find a whole new
bright-light big-city, or I'll smack 'em without pity.

If you wanna stay in my space, better keep
outa my face. I don't wanna see you within
eyeshot, constantly interrupting trains of thought,

climbing over Bostich and Faber Castel, mooning Fellowes,
Bic, Avery and Dell; darting, landing...HEY!! Bum!...
You just played hell!

-ruffled in Kentucky 1994

ಬಿಯೂಲ

Why Is It,

cows don't moo just to moo,
cocks don't crow just to crow,
owls don't whoo just to whoo?

Horses won't neigh just to neigh,
even asses don't bray just to bray?

But DOGS... STU-PID, howling dogs
--fool, sleep-taking hogs--
mongrel and bitch and whelp-mutts
won't shut the ye-lp UP?!!

-irked in Kentucky

By Then

Always--I've noticed, reflecting in the early quietness,
as fog is peep-tomming at the windows, and leaving his
breathing on the glass—
It seems to be at *about the same time* that
anything significant has to happen...

..Like, waiting anxiously, drearily, dreading the passing of
thoughts-accelerated time, and getting closer to the moment
when you know the call has to come... whether you want it to
or not...

Then...at other times, while *praying* for time to hurry,
the gray fogged-moments silently drag in the earliness
like a trailing slug, until you will wait no longer, and you
decide, misty-eyed, you must act, by then, no matter what...

It's the same time, when the limit is set
on any inauspicious occasion happening at the moment...
the drunken fool who didn't find his way home last night,
will not be given a moment more past then,
before his clothes are thrown out into the yard...

Periodically, the expectant moment arrives ahead of time,
like an unexpected early, bawling baby,
but whatever has to happen, must happen by then.

...Peculiar...how that time keeps reappearing throughout life
in sacred-like importance.
like, having to be at the desk at that time...
if you're calling in--
better have your tale together before then...

-tripod shot, in the wee hours of the morning – 1995

Birds

I hate you,
you spiteful crapping birds
leaving latex white-out
melded to the car windows,
splatting the deck with fecal epoxy.
(Plunking the fake owl on the awning
screech-halted all deck chaise doodoo,
didn't it, Dodos?
Honestly, thought you'd figure it out
and finally just poop on its head,
but for three and a half seasons
you haven't dared. What birdbrains.
When I roof-plant the model
whose head rotates, you'll really crap).

I despise all of you defecating
backyard nest builders,
flying geese, charging chickens,
and puffing country turkeys.

Utmost high loathing to
the slimy-excretion-shooting crows
who take to the air in unison
from the bell tower,
blacken the sky, and mass-bomb
the running, shrieking campus;
who commandeer park trees
and shrew to high heaven,
as nervous passers-by bolt past;
and during reconnaissance,
squadron-lift and blitz entire downtown blocks;
sidewalks, steps, benches, parking lots;
the entire world,
        a slippery, yellow-dysentery, mucousy mess.

I abhor your fricking feather flopping;
don't venture near while I'm picnicking,
or dining on the avenue,
I quease, and want to hurl.

But your resonance...
awakening at first-light dawn,
to communal greeting and calling,
bird fights over the bathroom and newspaper,
and arguing throughout breakfast
along the neighboring streets,
the twurgles and wurples, and churgles and chirps
...assuring, comforting clamor.

In the oncoming eve,
as trees come alive with the
songs of birds returning from soccer games,
and over-talking guests at the dinner table,
chattering on the phones,
and winding down for bed...
as with crickets, ocean surf
and rain on the roof,
the most pleasant, soothing din
on earth.
...Except for the low, deceitful cooings
of gray-mound-squirting,
ledge lounging pigeons.
I detest them.

- home and town- 1993

⟡

Faster Than We Imagined

We are the "old people" we used to look at with age fright;
the dental-partialed mouths that would never be our plight;
the way-one-day that was years and things away.

We are the chicken-legged, heave-bust parents of our friends;
the crow's-feet lined and the jowled slack-chinned;
we are what it would take us "forever and never" to be.

We are the age when our chic clothes split our children's sides;
we are the joint-achy and the truck-butt wide,
...and we got here faster than a peregrine swoop.

-time-lapse photo – 1995

www.ingramcontent.com/pod-product-compliance
Lightning Source LLC
LaVergne TN
LVHW022318080426
835509LV00036B/2582